Wolves

By Nora May

Library For All Ltd.

Library For All is an Australian not for profit organisation with a mission to make knowledge accessible to all via an innovative digital library solution. Visit us at www.libraryforall.org.au

Wolves

First published 2019

Published by Library For All Ltd
Email: info@libraryforall.org.au
URL: http://www.libraryforall.org.au

PNGAus Partnership

This book was produced by the Together For Education Partnership supported by the Australian Government through the Papua New Guinea-Australia Partnership.

Wolves
May, Nora
ISBN: 978-1-925932-53-9

Images sourced from Pixabay.com, Unsplash.com, Wikimedia.org, Freepik.com under a CCO license.

A wolf is a type of canine. They are the largest animals in the dog family.

Wolves live in Europe, Asia and North America. They live in many different environments, including deserts, grasslands, mountains and the taiga.

The taiga, or snow forest, is the largest land biome in the world. A biome is a community of plants and animals. The taiga has lots of trees and space for wolves to live.

Wolves are very social animals. They live in groups called packs. The leader of the pack is called the alpha.

Baby wolves are called pups. They cannot see when they are born. Their eyes change colour from blue to yellow when they are around 10 weeks old.

Wolves live for up to 8 years in the wild, although they can live longer in captivity.

Wolves have sharp teeth and powerful jaws. They can open their jaws wider than other types of dog.

Wolves are carnivores. This means they eat meat. They hunt other animals in packs and share their catch.

Wolves can travel long distances to find food. They can walk for a whole day without resting. They are also good swimmers.

Wolves communicate with other wolves by howling. Wolves can hear each other from very far away. Wolves have very good hearing. They can hear high pitched sounds that humans cannot hear.

Some species of wolves are endangered. In some areas wolves are hunted for the fur. In other regions, their habitats are being destroyed by humans.

It is important that we look after the environment so that wolves have space to live.

What is your favourite fact about this amazing animal?

About The Author

St Columba Animal Series

This book series was written by 4th grade students at St Columba School in Durango, Colorado, with support from Library For All.

The Library For All team ran workshops alongside teaching staff to encourage students and their families to get involved in the book creation process. Students were taught how to research information about animals and how to prepare a book draft for editing.

Library For All works in partnership with authors and illustrators all over the world to create a unique digital library.

www.ingramcontent.com/pod-product-compliance
Lightning Source LLC
Chambersburg PA
CBHW040314050426
42452CB00018B/2842